Samuel Hopkins Emery

A Memorial of the Congregational Ministers and Churches of

the Illinois

Association, on Completing a Quarter of a Century of its History

Samuel Hopkins Emery

A Memorial of the Congregational Ministers and Churches of the Illinois
Association, on Completing a Quarter of a Century of its History

ISBN/EAN: 9783337013646

Printed in Europe, USA, Canada, Australia, Japan

Cover: Foto ©ninafisch / pixelio.de

More available books at **www.hansebooks.com**

A MEMORIAL

OF THE

CONGREGATIONAL MINISTERS AND CHURCHES

OF THE

ILLINOIS ASSOCIATION,

ON

COMPLETING A QUARTER OF A CENTURY OF ITS HISTORY,

CONSISTING OF A

COMMEMORATIVE DISCOURSE,

By Rev. WILLIAM CARTER, of Pittsfield,

AN ORIGINAL MEMBER,

DELIVERED AT QUINCY, OCT. 26, 1860;

AND AN

HISTORICAL APPENDIX.

———•◆•———

COMPILED BY REV. S. HOPKINS EMERY.

———•◆•———

QUINCY, ILL.:

WHIG AND REPUBLICAN STEAM POWER PRESS, 38 FOURTH STREET.

1863.

INTRODUCTORY NOTICE.

The following extracts from the minutes of the Illinois Association will explain the appearance of this publication. At its meeting in Newtown, in April 1860, it was "voted, that the next meeting be held with the First Church of Quincy. Inasmuch as a quarter of a century has already passed since a Convention was held in that place, resulting in the organization of this Association, therefore, on motion of Bro. Emery, Resolved, that Rev. WILLIAM CARTER, one of the original members, be requested to prepare an Historical Discourse." It was also "voted, that Bro. Emery be requested to make other suitable arrangements for it, as a *Commemorative Meeting.*"

The meeting was held in Quincy, Oct. 25th, 26th and 27th, 1860. The Historical Discourse of Bro. Carter was preached on Friday evening, Oct. 26th. Interesting Reminiscences were given by Rev. Messrs. Edward Beecher and E. Jenney, of Galesburg, and Rev. Asa Turner, of Denmark, Io., Rev. Horatio Foote, of Quincy, and Dea. J. Chittenden, of Mendon, who were early on the ground, and some of whom were connected with the Association at the beginning.

On Saturday, the 27th, the following resolutions were moved by Bro. Emery, and unanimously adopted :

"The Illinois Association, convened, after a quarter of a century, in the place where it first was organized, desires to record its views in the following resolutions :

" *Resolved,* 1. That we re-affirm the great principles of civil and religious liberty, which the Fathers of New England and the Founders of its Congregational Churches labored so faithfully and effectually to inculcate and disseminate. We rejoice in these principles, as alive to-day, suited to our time, adapted to all ages, and every place—West as well as East.

" *Resolved,* 2. That the review of the last twenty-five years, reveals such a multiplication of Churches, and opening of new fields of labor to our denomination, as call for devout gratitude to God, who hath hitherto so abundantly blessed us. Encouraged and incited by past experience of the divine goodness, to fresh activity in the work of Christ, the purpose is hereby solemnly avowed of a more complete consecration to that work, in the effort of multiplying the number of true disciples, to spread the knowledge and extend the practice of a pure gospel.

" *Resolved,* 3. That for the benefit of those who may come after us, as well as to serve the present age, a Committee of this Association be appointed, whose duty it shall be, to secure the collection, and, so soon as the necessary funds can be raised, the publication of such historical matter, as may come within their reach, tending to illustrate the life, and honor the memory of deceased members of this Association, and to interpret and extend the views and aims of this Body, and lay by in store a rich repository of facts for the time to come.

" *Resolved*, 4. That the thanks of this Association be extended to Rev. Mr. Carter, for his Historical Discourse, and a copy of the same be requested for publication in the proposed printed memorial of this Body."

The Committee, proposed in the third resolution, was appointed, consisting of Rev. Messrs. Hawley, Emery, Coltrine, Carter, and Dea. Chittenden.

The committee subsequently reported to the Association, at its meeting in Mendon, May, 1861, and its materials in hand were committed to Rev. Messrs. Emery, Foote, and Dea. Chittenden, for publication.

This publication has been delayed for nearly two years, chiefly on account of the multiplicity of other engagements, but partially for the reason that no person has cared to assume the pecuniary liability. That person, however, has now been found in the enterprising publisher of the Quincy Whig and Republican, who has already secured his paper and is asking for copy.

Just returned from a visit of several weeks among the Hospitals and Army of the Southwest, it is a pleasant change, and not unwelcome relaxation from the fatigue and toil of such a trip, to brush away the dust from long neglected manuscripts, and commune with the men of other days, ere the clash of arms, and rude clamor of the present distracted times, disturbed the peace, and interrupted the friendly communion of sister States.

To the Great Head of the Church, this endeavor to preserve the history of a small portion of one branch of that Church, is commended, with the hope it may excite, with all its imperfections, to a like work elsewhere.

S. HOPKINS EMERY.

Quincy, Ill., January, 1863.

MEMORIAL.

COMMEMORATIVE DISCOURSE.

DEUT. 8: 2.—"*And thou shalt remember all the way which the Lord thy God led thee.*"

This language was addressed to the ancient people of Israel. It is also proper for individuals and communities, as well as nations, to remember all the way in which the Lord their God hath led them. So is it for churches, denominations, and the whole church of Christ, to remember the way in which their Redeemer hath led them. The natural tendency of such reminiscence is to increase our fidelity and devotion to Him.

Having been appointed by our local Association to prepare a Historical Discourse, in respect to Congregationalism in Illinois, I shall proceed at once to the work assigned me.

The first Congregational Church, organized in Illinois, was at Mendon in Adams County, Feb. 1833. This was not, however, the first Congregational Church in the State. There was a Congregational Church organized in Massachusetts, March, 1831, composed of a Colony, which came to Princeton, Illinois. The history of this Church has been less known, from its having occupied an independent position, and not having reported itself to our General Association, until 1857. We have been accustomed, therefore, to regard the Church at Mendon as the first in the State, as it was, in fact, the first Church organized here. This Church at Mendon was formed in the cabin of Deacon J. B. Chittenden. A sermon was preached, and the Lord's Supper administered, by Rev. SOLOMON HARDY. The furniture, at the communion, was a junk bottle and tumbler. The pulpit was a puncheon table. It was a season of interest;—

perhaps of as great spiritual refreshment as they ever enjoyed. Undoubtedly the Saviour's promised presence cheered their hearts. The Church was originally composed of eighteen members. Deacon Chittenden and wife, and another lady, are the only surviving members of the original Church. It now numbers one hundred and twenty members, and has long been self-sustaining.

The second Congregational Church, organized in this State, was at Quincy, Oct. 10, 1833. It had been a Presbyterian Church, formed about three years before. Rev. Asa Turner, now of Iowa, was its pastor—one of the most devoted and useful ministers in the West; and who, more than any other man, may be regarded as the father of Congregationalism in Illinois and Iowa. Deacon Chittenden, who came to Quincy in the fall of 1831, and was made a ruling elder in the Presbyterian Church, of that place, was invited to be present and counsel with them, at the re-organization of the Church on the Congregational plan.

The third Congregational Church, organized in Illinois, was at Jacksonville, Dec. 15th, 1833, about two months after the organization of the Church at Quincy. President Sturtevant, of Illinois College and myself, assisted in the organization. This Church was composed originally of about thirty members. I was invited to take the pastoral care of it, contrary to my expectation and wish, for I had a preference for Pioneer labor, on which I had just entered. Reluctantly I took charge of it for nearly five years, during which time it increased from thirty to about one hundred members.

I may here say that when I came to this State in the Autumn of 1833, I had no other thought than that of laboring entirely in the Presbyterian Church, and to build up Presbyterian Churches. The Presbyterians had, as they claimed, possession of the ground, and I had no other wish than that they should retain it, exclusively, so far as Congregationalism was concerned. But one of the first things I found, after coming to the State, was that Congregationalists from New England claimed the right to form Churches of their own order, where they could do so, without interfering with Presbyterians—that where a place was large enough for two self-sustaining Churches, one might be Congregational, if the brethren preferred it; and, that in organizing a Church in a new place, the majority of the members had a right to decide whether it should be Congregational or Presbyterian. This claim seemed so obviously just, that I could but at once accede to it, and adopt it. I made up my mind, that in such cases, when desired, I would assist in organizing Congregational churches. This was the only ground I ever had occasion to maintain on this subject, and it was so reasonable that our Presbyterian friends soon yielded it. And, as a matter of fact, it has been my happiness, for the most part, to be on the most friendly terms with our Presbyterian brethren, and to co-operate as frequently and cordially with brethren in the Presbyterian connection, as in the Congregational.— Both denominations, Congregationalists and New School Presbyterians, early concurred in the important principle, that where there was already a Congregational or Presbyterian Church, in a place not able to sustain two Churches, it was not expedient to divide and form another Church.— Within the bounds of our local Association, there has been but a single exception on each side. Both were, perhaps, regarded as peculiar cases. But as confession of our own faults is more becoming than those of our neighbors, I will say, that in my own judgment, it would have been far better that the exception had not been made by us. Much evil and no good, I think, has been the result of it. I have dwelt thus upon this principle because I think it a very important item in the history of our denomination in this part of the State.

I will now speak of the fourth Congregational Church organized in this part of the State—that at Griggsville, Aug. 1834. Rev. Asa Turner, of Quincy, and myself, held a meeting of several days in Griggsville, and organized a Church of twelve members. Small as this Church was, such were the differences among the members, that it was thought expedient, by some of them, for the sake of peace, to organize another Congregational Church by its side.   In a short time, however, through the influence of other christians, who came there to reside, another Church was formed uniting all the members of the two.   This Church has grown to be one of the strongest and most prosperous of our denomination in the State.

In the early part of Nov., 1834, Rev. Mr. Turner and myself went to Atlas to hold a protracted meeting, by invitation of the principal citizens of the place.   There was not only no Church in the region, but no professor of religion to make a prayer at a funeral.   Several members of Mr. Turner's Church accompanied him, and rendered important aid in the meeting. One of the first things we discovered, and the most discouraging, was that almost every one we met, was in the habit of drinking intoxicating liquor.   Of this we had evidence we could not resist, though we saw no one intoxicated.   But we had been taught that there was little hope of success in preaching the gospel to those who were under the influence of intoxicating drink.   The question arose, whether we had not better form a Temperance Society before proceeding farther.   We proposed this question to one of our friends, who had invited us there, and who was our host.   He told us we had better try the efficacy of the gospel.   And he was right.*   We had good, attentive audiences to the close.   At the last meeting, Sabbath night, wishing to know whether there was any religious interest, we invited any, who desired to have religious conversation with us, to remain after the congregation was dismissed.   To our surprise, one of those who remained, was Capt. Leonard Ross, one of the most influential men in the neighborhood.   I shall never forget my sensations on that occasion.   I seemed to myself but a youth, being in the first year of my ministry.   This man of large stature, of a great heart, and a noble intellect, came and sat down by my side on a low bench, and asked me if I could tell him what to do to

*This was Col. W. Ross, who did not, as we had hoped, profess at that time to yield to the power of the gospel, but did afterwards, at Pittsfield, where he removed, and built a house of worship, costing from four to five thousand dollars, and gave it, with the lot and bell, to the Congregational Church of that place.

become a Christian. I was overwhelmed with wonder and joy. I tried to tell him what to do, and he did not wait until the next morning before he did it. He was a burning and a shining light in the community for nearly two years, and then went to Heaven.

He organized a Temperance Society, and exerted a temperance influence which, perpetuated by his son-in-law, Lyman Scott, made that region one of the most temperate in the county—perhaps in the State. His Christian life is still an example to all who knew him.

After his conversion, he told me he had been a skeptic, and in the habit of drinking a large quantity of ardent spirits every day. He had no thought of attending the meeting, but was over-persuaded by his wife to come. At the first meeting, he came to the very sober conclusion that the preaching would do him no good while drinking at that rate. He therefore made up his mind to drink no more during the meeting. At the very next meeting he attended, his infidelity was swept away, and an arrow from the hand of God was fastened in his soul, which resulted in his conversion. Others were hopefully converted during the meetings, and soon after a small Congregational Church was formed, of which he was the main pillar. He took a minister, Rev. Warren Nichols, into his house, and with the aid of his two brothers, principally supported him. The Church still continues, now known as the Congregational Church of Rockport and Summer Hill —originally, the Congregational Church of Rockport and Atlas.

Having five Congregational Churches in this part of the State, it was thought best to have them united in an Association for mutual helpfulness and co-operation. Accordingly a meeting was held for this purpose, at Quincy, the latter part of November, 1834—the same month with the meeting at Atlas. Four of the Churches were represented by delegates, viz: the Churches of Mendon, Quincy, Jacksonville and Griggsville. There were but two ministers present—Mr. Turner and myself—both of us members of Schuyler Presby-

2

tery. The former had united with it, having charge of a
Presbyterian Church, and I had united with it to be ordained,
as the only alternative at that time to going to New England
for ordination. This was before the division of the Presbyterian Church into New and Old School. At this first meeting at Quincy, a draft of a Constitution, Articles of Faith and
By-Laws was agreed upon, to be submitted to the Churches
for their action, to be reported at the next meeting, to be held
in Jacksonville the following year, October, 1835.

At the meeting in Jacksonville, all five of the Churches
were represented—Rev. Warren Nichols, of Atlas, also being
present. The Churches reported their acceptance of the Constitution and Articles of Faith, some of them suggesting
amendments. The Articles were revised, amended and
adopted.

The Association, I suppose it is well understood, is avow-
edly only an advisory Body, claiming no authoritative con-
trol whatever over the Churches. It is merely a bond of union
for mutual aid, and the better promotion of the Redeemer's
Kingdom. It is an Association of Churches and Ministers.
It was felt to be important among other things, that we should
have some Ecclesiastical Body to license and ordain ministers
of the Gospel. The Association has answered an important
end in this respect. A special meeting was called the next
Spring, for the purpose of ordaining Rev. Julius A. Reed,
now of Iowa. At this special meeting, several ministers
united with the Association.

At the meeting in Jacksonville, Oct., 1835, there was pres-
ent Rev. Alfred Greenwood, representing the Congregational
Union of Fox River. In June, 1835, three Congregational
Churches in the Fox River country, and one in Indiana, at
Michigan city, held a convention for the purpose of forming
an Association, to be called the Fox River Union. The three
Churches of this State were at Dupage, (now Naperville,) at
Big Grove, LaSalle county, and at Walker's Grove, Cook
county. Only the first two exist at present—the first organ-
ized in August, the other in November, 1834.

In the year 1835, there were but ten Congregational Churches in the State—five in our Association, called the Congregational Association of Illinois—three in Fox River Union—one at Princeton, and one at Batavia, organized August, 1835.

In 1836, there were nine more Congregational Churches organized in the State, five of them in this part of the State, which united with our Association, viz: the Churches of Round Prairie, (near Plymouth,) Payson, LaHarpe, Carthage and Waverly.

It may be proper here to say, that the Congregational Churches of this State at first took the broad ground of Christian union—that we would receive to our communion all those we have reason to believe the Lord Jesus Christ had received, if they wished to unite with us—that the only condition of membership should be credible evidence of Christian character. The Articles of Faith which we required those uniting with us to assent to, were only the fundamental doctrines which all Evangelical Churches hold in common. Indeed, this was the ground taken by the early Congregationalists of New England, as abundantly shown by Dr. Hawes, in his Tribute to the Memory of the Pilgrims. And this was the character of the Articles of Faith in the only Churches I was connected with in New England—the Church in Yale College, and the First Congregational Church in Hartford, of which Dr. Hawes is pastor.

The result has been, that Christians of different Evangelical denominations have united with us and dwelt together in harmony, so far as doctrines were concerned. I do not say that other Evangelical denominations have not practically adopted essentially the same principle in this Western country. I think they have, for it commends itself to every one as a true principle, that those who are good enough for the Lord Jesus Christ are good enough for us. Neither the Old nor the New School Presbyterians, I believe, require the lay members to assent to all the doctrines of the Confession of Faith, but only to a summary embracing the fundamentals.

If the different denominations are not to be united in form, as they may never be, it is much to be desired that they may be united in heart, under our Great Leader, to accomplish the common object, the salvation of the world. And whatever may be the appearance of things at times, I presume every Christian can testify that there has been a real advance in the spirit of Christian union within his recollection.

As appears from the foregoing, there were nineteen Congregational Churches in Illinois in 1836. For the next eight years they increased at an average of five in a year, when in 1844 there were about sixty churches of our order in the State. In that year, 1844, a General Association for the State was formed at Farmington. There were present at that meeting six ministers—Rev. Messrs. J. T. Holmes, R. M. Pearson, M. N. Miles, L. H. Parker, John Cross and myself, and about as many Churches were represented. This General Association has proved, as it was intended to be, a bond of union for all the Churches of our denomination in the State. There are now one hundred and ninety-five Congregational Churches connected with the General Association through the local Associations. In 1844, at the time of the organization of the General Association, there were but two local Associations in the State—the Illinois Association and Fox River Union. Now there are ten local Associations.

The increase of Congregational Churches has been gradual; probably about in proportion to the increase of population in the State. From 1833 to 1844, the increase was about five in a year, on an average. From 1844 to 1854, about six in a year. From 1854 to 1860, about ten in a year. The greatest number organized in any one year, was nineteen in 1858. There were eleven organized in 1854 and 1857 each.

It is said there are known to be eleven Congregational Churches in the State unassociated—making the whole number of Congregational Churches in Illinois more than two hundred. It is believed this is considerably greater than the number of either New or Old School Presbyterian Churches in the State.

Thus the number has been increased beyond the most sanguine expectations of those who organized the first Congregational Churches in the State twenty-seven years ago. But this is no occasion for pride or boasting, but for thankfulness rather, as we remember all the way the Lord, our God, has led us for nearly thirty years. It thus becomes evident that our denomination has a work to do in this State, and is permitted to stand by the side of the other Protestant, Evangelical denominations, in promoting the common cause of our Redeemer here and through the world. Our true position is not one of antagonism towards any of these denominations. We are rather so many brigades under one Great Commander, marching to the accomplishment of a common object. Nor are we like the different parties in politics, each of which, while they all profess to have the same end in view, the good of the country, holds that the other is pursuing a course subversive of the professed end. We hold that each of these Protestant, Evangelical denominations, is using means adapted to the common end—the Sword of the Spirit against the common enemy, and that each is contending successfully— that while there may be some difference in their uniforms and tactics and internal regulations, each perhaps is pursuing the course best fitted for its own success. At least it is lawful for each company to be its own judge, and for each individual to choose in which company he will enlist as a soldier of Christ.

Let each one fulfill his part in the ranks where his lot is cast, and he may expect to contribute his quota to the final victory, and hear his Lord say of him, *Well done, good and faithful servant.*

NOTE BY THE COMPILER.

Deacon Chittenden, of whom frequent mention is made in the preceding discourse, has been recently called home to his rest and reward in Heaven. He was present at the Commemorative Meeting in Quincy, and interested the people with his reminiscences of early times. He was appointed to assist in the publication of this memorial, so long delayed, but his valuable counsel and aid are denied us. It is due to the memory of such a valued friend, to place on record the following brief notice, the principal items of which were furnished by his Pastor, Rev. Mr. Campbell:

Deacon Chittenden was born in Guilford, Conn., March, 1790, of pious parents. He had good opportunities for education, and taught school in the East. When quite young, he was chosen Deacon of the Church, and was an active laborer in the cause of Christ. Father Turner, President Sturtevant, and other young men in Yale College, came West, and the letters of the former led Deacon Chittenden to follow him. He left Guilford in September, 1831, and reached Quincy in December of the same year, after a most fatiguing journey. A leading motive with Deacon Chittenden in his removal, was the prospect of greater usefulness.— Uniting with what is now the First Congregational Church in Quincy the 17th of December, 1831, he was soon chosen Elder, (for it was then styled a Presbyterian Church,) which office he accepted March 3d, 1832. He was well skilled in singing, and is said to have taught the first Singing School in the Military Tract. It was early in 1832, Deacon Chittenden proposed a settlement in the present town of Mendon, establishing a Sabbath School, and securing other religious services. As the result of this, a Congregational Church was organized in February of the following year, the first in the State, organized on the ground. Chosen Deacon at this time, he retained the office, and fulfilled faithfully its duties, till he died. For several years, he acted as Agent of the American Sunday School Union, planting Sabbath Schools, and performing the work of an Evangelist, acceptable and useful in all this region, a man of strict integrity, whose praise is in all the Churches. All pronounced him an honest, heavenly minded, laborious man of God, ever ready for the coming of his Lord. His death, sudden at last, occurred January 23, 1863, in his 74th year. His estimable wife had been called home a short time before, as if to make him the more ready to follow.

HISTORICAL APPENDIX.

1. *Notice of the Congregational Church in Barry, Pike County, Illinois, by Br. G. G.* SHIPMAN, *member.*—The Church in Barry was organized February 7th, 1846, with eleven members. Rev. William C. Merritt, first Pastor, labored with the Church until July, 1849. The ministry of the second Pastor, Rev. C. S. Cady, continued from Dec., 1850, to the Spring of 1853. Rev. George J. Barrett commenced his labors, January, 1855, supplying the pulpit for half the time, two years. Rev. Z. K. Hawley supplied the pulpit from January to November, 1858. Rev. S. T. Babbitt preached from January to June, 1859. Rev. George W. Williams commenced his labors, January, 1860, and closed with the year.

The Church have built a good house of worship, costing fifteen hundred dollars, and are out of debt.

2. *Notice of the Church in Beverly, Adams county, Illinois, by Rev.* GEORGE W. WILLIAMS, *Minister.*—This Church was organized Dec. 27th, 1859, with seventeen members. The Council called for this purpose was composed of the following Pastors :

1st Church, Quincy, Rev. S. H. Emery ; Cong. Church, Macomb, Rev. Z. K. Hawley ; Cong. Church, Payson, Rev. C. A. Leach ; Cong. Church, Griggsville, Rev. N. P. Coltrin.

The following Churches were represented by lay delegates : Congregational Church, Payson, L. Faxon ; Cong. Church, Hannibal, Wm. H. Ide ; Cong. Church, Barry, G. G. Shipman.

Rev. Z. K. Hawley was chosen Moderator, and Br. Wm.

H. Ide, Secretary. Rev. N. P. Coltrin preached, by request, in the afternoon, a sermon on Congregationalism. Rev. S. H. Emery, by invitation, preached in the evening. Rev. Z. K. Hawley charged and counselled the Church. Rev. C. A. Leach expressed the Fellowship of the Churches. It was one of the most profitable and pleasant of Council meetings.

3. *Notice of the Church in Canton, Lewis county, Missouri, by Rev. S. Hopkins Emery, one of the Council who organized it.*—The Congregational Church in Canton, Mo., is composed of Germans, and was organized the 7th of June, 1860, thirty persons, principally heads of families, covenanting together, with a Calvinistic Confession of Faith, and professing to be regenerate. By request, Rev. S. H. Emery, of Quincy, preached on the occasion, and other services were conducted in German. This was the third Congregational Church organized in Missouri. The present minister is Rev. Abraham Frowein, formerly of Iowa, who has been with them nearly from the beginning, and with good unanimity on the part of the people.

4. *Notice of the Church in Carthage, Hancock county, Illinois, by Br. Samuel A. Newhall, member.*—The Congregational Church in Carthage was organized in March, 1836. It has been supplied with preaching by Rev. Messrs. Benj. F. Morris, Joseph Mason, James A. Hawley, William E. Catlin and William B. Atkinson, till 1857, since which time it has been destitute of a minister, and its members have worshipped with other congregations. The meeting house is rented for school purposes. There are some ten or fifteen members who have not taken letters to other churches. It is hoped that, some day, there may be such an increase of population as will bring up the Church. The trustees are G. W. Batchelder, J. W. Hawley and Samuel A. Newhall.

5. *Notice of the Church in Cedron, Hancock county, Illinois, by Br. Dudley B. Eells, member.*—The Church in Cedron was organized May 24th, 1854.* The original number of

---

* The date in the minutes of General Association is 1856. We give 1854, on the supposition it is or should be correct.

members was thirteen. Our first minister was Rev. N. P. Coltrin, whose labors commenced Oct., 1853, and ended Oct., 1857. Our second and present minister is Rev. Samuel Dilley, who commenced his labors in March, 1858.

The Church has labored under the disadvantage of having no place of worship, except small and inconvenient school houses. Its members are mostly heads of families, whose homes are near together.

6. *Notice of the Church in Dallas City, Hancock county, Illinois, by Rev.* ANDREW L. PENNOYER, *Minister.*—The Congregational Church of Dallas City was organized in a revival of religion, January 17th, 1859, with nineteen members, by Rev. Wm. Salter, of Burlington, and Andrew L. Pennoyer, of LaHarpe. Though some were members of other churches, all came in on Profession of Faith, viz: George H. Ames, Mrs. Frances Ames, Henry F. Black, Mrs. Mary N. Black, Thomas C. Patterson, Mrs. Catharine E. Patterson, John F. Thomas, Mrs. Jane Thomas, Mrs. Marietta Rollosson, Stephen Jackson, Miss Sarah Jackson, John D. Jackson, Mrs. Elizabeth Jackson, Lyman B. Rand, Miss Diantha McMullen, Miss Amanda Sayres, Miss Rachel Ann Sayres, Miss Emma Stoops, Mrs. Julia M. Bryan.

At the time of the organization of this Church, no organized church of any name was found here. During the following summer, a neat brick house of worship was erected, 80 feet by 45, walls 18 feet high, with a stone basement. We have had three revivals of religion, and have received sixty-four, in all, to the Church. We have dismissed twenty to other churches. We now number forty-four. Our Sabbath School numbers sixty. I moved my family here in the fall of 1860, although I had preached here, half the time, for more than two years. Our attendance on the Sabbath is seventy-five to one hundred and upwards.

7. *Notice of the German Congregational Church in Fall Creek, Adams county, Illinois, by Rev.* CHARLES EDWARD CONRAD, *Minister.*—Fall Creek, twelve miles from Quincy, the most neglected and perhaps depraved region, far or near,

attracted me at once, so soon as I had arrived in Quincy, and made it my duty to go there, and preach to the scattered all about, the sweet and blessed Gospel. It was a hard and wild soil, and only by long suffering, and perseverance, I succeeded at last, to get them first, and for three years, together in private houses, in regular meetings, until, under the greatest difficulties and embarrassments, on every side, Rev. Br. S. H. Emery, Deacon Willard Keyes and myself organized, Dec. 3d, 1860, a Congregational Church, consisting of nineteen members, bearing the name of the German Congregational Church of Fall Creek, Adams county, Illinois.

We, by the blessing of God, continue since, having built, in 1861, a meeting house of stone, on land donated by Messrs. Bushnell and Browning, of Quincy, and having received into the church relation, on profession of their faith, seven members more. Two of our number have removed to other places, so that our total membership at present is twenty-four.

This little flock proves a blessing to the whole vicinity, and though much despised and hated, yet the desert and the wilderness, in their young offspring as well as the old, drink up the gentle rain, and honey dew of the Gospel graces bestowed upon them in the Divine services, and Sabbath School, and it is hoped the Lord will let us prosper, though it may be first in some future time.

8. *Notice of the Church in Griggsville, Pike county, Illinois, by Rev. N. P. Coltrin, Minister.*—I have consulted the Church record to give the facts as to the Ministers of this place. In some cases I give the date at which the Minister is first or last named as Moderator of Church meeting, as ministering to the Church:

1. A. T. Norton,* Feb. 1, 1837, Feb. 23, 1838—1 year
2. Wm. Whittlesey, June 15, 1838, Oct. 19, 1838—3 months.
3. A. L. Pennoyer, Dec. 28, 1838, (installed Aug. 8, 1839,) April 26, 1840—1 year, 3 months.

* NOTE BY REV. WILLIAM CARTER.—Rev. Edward Hollister was minister of the Griggsville Church before Mr. Norton. He was their first minister.

4. J. Ballard, May 7, 1841, Jan. 23, 1843—1 year, 6 months.
5. J. T. Holmes, Nov. 8, 1843, died April 13, 1847—3 years, 4 months.
6. W. H. Starr, Oct. 23, 1848, farewell sermon Sept. 29, 1850—2 years.
7. T. Lyman, Nov. 7, 1851, Nov., 1852—1 year.
8. R. Mears, Feb. 20, 1853, (installed April 18, 1853,) died March 28, 1856—3 years,
9. W. Herritt, Jan., 1857, April 1857—3 months.
10. N. P. Coltrin,*†Sept. 11, 1857, Feb., 1861—3 years, 5 months.

Two hundred and ten have been added to the Church by profession, one hundred ane sixty-three by letter, making a sum total of three hundred and seventy-three, of whom ninety-eight have been dismissed to other churches, twenty-five have died, and eighteen have been excluded, leaving two hundred and thirty-two, whilst the actual membership is only about two hundred. The difference is owing to the fact that for some time the deaths were not recorded, or that members have slipped out and disappeared in some unrecorded ways.

9. *Notice of the Church in Hamilton, Hancock county, Illinois, by Br.* EDWARD F. HUMPHREY, *member.*—The First Congregational Church of Hamilton was organized May 19th, 1859. This was done at the request of fifteen persons, who composed, at that time, its entire number. Feeling that Hamilton was a growing town, and that it was their duty as Christians thus to lay a foundation for present and future usefulness, they went forward in this enterprise. Three of these persons brought letters from the Montebello Church, four from the First Congregational Church of Quincy, one from the Presbyterian Church of Warsaw, one was received by profession, and the remaining number were from different places, Churches and States, East.

For two years after its organization, this Church was without a minister only as temporary arrangements supplied it, a few Sabbaths at a time. During this period, however, a regular weekly prayer meeting was sustained, and one person was received by profession into the Church. Repeated efforts were made to secure a minister as a permanent supply, but

* Rev. Mr. Coltrin has left, and his place is supplied by Rev. William W. Whipple, for many years minister of a Presbyterian Church in La Grange, Missouri.

all were unsuccessful. The commercial prostration of the place was so great that instead of that increase in its population which had been expected, it diminished.

About the middle of May, 1861, the Rev. E. N. Bartlett came to this place, and after a short visit, an engagement was made with him to become the pastor of the Church for one year. Mr. Bartlett is still its pastor, and the Church is increasing. Seven have been received into it since he entered this field of labor. Three have been dismissed by letter since the formation of the Church, and the record now shows its number to be twenty.

This Church has never completed its organization by electing proper officers, such as Deacons and Trustees, but it is intending to do so soon. At the present time its only officer is a clerk.

Ten of the members of this Church are laborers in the Union Sabbath School established in this place, and which promises to be a blessing to all the Churches.

10. *Notice of the First Congregational Church in Hannibal, Marion county, Missouri, by Rev.* JULIAN M. STURTEVANT, JR., *Minister.*—This Church was formed by an Ecclesiastical Council, of which Rev. T. M. Post, of St. Louis, Mo., was Moderator, and Rev. S. H. Emery, of Quincy, Ill., was Scribe, on the 29th day of November, 1859, at which time it had twenty-four members. The Church edifice was begun in the following March, and was dedicated to the service of God on the 28th of June, 1860. At the same time the present pastor, Rev. J. M. Sturtevant, Jr., was ordained to the work of the ministry. Since then the history of the Church has contained few events of striking public interest. By the blessing of God, the number of its members has been doubled and its strength gradually increased. The position of the Church in reference to the rebellion and its great cause, subjected its members to great annoyances and considerable dangers in the early part of our national struggle; but the very positiveness of this position has entirely saved it from those internal dissensions which have torn nearly all the Churches.

of the State, and as the struggle has advanced, has secured
to it the confidence of all those in the community whose good
opinion is most desirable. From its present position, this
young Church has a good right to look forward to many generations of usefulness in a large field as yet almost' entirely
unoccupied by Congregationalism.

NOTE BY THE COMPILER.—A letter just received from the
pastor of this Church, dated March 7th, 1863, states: "We
receive thirty-three to the Church to-morrow. More than
half of them are heads of families. The Lord's name be
praised!"

11. *Notice of the Church in Hillsgrove, McDonough county,
Illinois, by Rev. WILLIAM A. CHAMBERLIN, Minister of the
Round Prairie Church, Plymonth.*—This Church was organized in 1841. Its ministers have been Rev. Messrs. E. E.
Murdock, D. R. Williams and —— Nichols. By deaths, dis-
missals and removals, the Church has become nearly, if not
quite extinct. In its early history, it was instrumental of
much good, and especially the school, which one of its principal members, Mr. Isaac Holton, founded, was greatly blessed
by the influences of the Holy Spirit, and many young men
were converted, who are now active Christians elsewhere.

12. *Notice of the German Congregational Church in La
Grange, Lewis county, Missouri, by Rev. S. HOPKINS EMERY,
one of the Council who organized it.*—By request of some
twenty persons, chiefly heads of families, Rev. Messrs. C. E.
Conrad and S. H. Emery, on behalf of the Churches of which
they are pastors, visited LaGrange, Mo., and assisted in organizing a German Congregational Church, consisting of such
as had adopted a Scriptural Confession of Faith, and who
gave evidence of a renewed state. The organization took
place Sept. 28th, 1861, and Rev. Abraham Frowein, minister
of the Church in Canton, Mo., has supplied them since that
date, with increasing signs of acceptance and usefulness.

13. *Notice of the Church in LaHarpe, Hancock county, Illinois, by Rev. WILLIAM B. ATKINSON, Minister.*—I have
taken considerable pains to obtain the dates of historic events

connected with this Church, but can do no better than to copy accurately from the "Records":

"March, 1836.—LaHarpe Congregational Church was organized March, 1836, consisting of sixteen members."

"March 22, 1848.—It was deemed necessary, for various reasons, to re-organize the Congregational Church of La-Harpe. * * * * Meetings were held at the house of the pastor, Rev. W. Nichols, for this purpose. The Christian character of those present being satisfactory to each other, it was voted to organize themselves into a Congregational Church. Articles of faith and covenant were adopted."

"April 9, 1848.—After sermon, the following individuals rose and acknowledged, in the presence of the congregation, the articles of faith previously adopted, and entered into covenant, viz:

Sam'l Hutton,	Mrs. L. C. Maynard,
Henry Bliss,	" Henry Comstock,
Lewis C. Maynard,	" W. A. Nichols,
. Lauren Tuttle,	" S. W. Nudd,
Wm. Leavitt,	" H. Bliss,
Henry Comstock,	" L. Tuttle.

* * * Lord's Supper. * * *

Attest: WARREN NICHOLS, *Acting Pastor.*"

"April 27, 1848.—L. C. Maynard was chosen Deacon."

Since the organization of the Church, the following ministers have labored in connection with it: William P. Apthorp, Z. K. Hawley, James A. Hawley, D. R. Williams, William Rankin, —— Perkins, F. Babbitt, Warren Nichols, J. H. Henry, T. H. Johnson, Andrew L. Pennoyer and William B. Atkinson. Rev. Mr. Johnson remained with the Church six years. He accepted a call for settlement, April 20, 1852, and preached his farewell sermon May 19, 1858. In 1853, steps were taken toward "building." Trustees were appointed, and aid of $250,00 from the Church building fund enabled them to complete the work.

14. *Notice of the Congregational Church in Macomb, Mc-Donough county, Illinois, by Rev. Z. K. HAWLEY, Minister.*—

This Church was organized Oct. 2, 1858, with twenty-four members. Hector M'Lean and Lorenzo Clisby were chosen Deacons. Rev. Z. K. Hawley commenced pastoral labors Nov. 8, 1858, and was installed April 18, 1859.

Arrangements were at first made for a place of worship by renting; but the experience of a few weeks showed the necessity of building. Within forty days from the vote to build, a small but neat chapel was erected, completed and dedicated, with some aid from abroad, chiefly from the Church Building Fund.

15. *Notice of the Congregational Church in Mendon, Adams county, Illinois, by Rev. A. B.* CAMPBELL, *Minister.*—The Church was organized by Rev. Solomon Hardy, in February, 1833. He supplied the Church till Rev. William Kirby was called, Jan. 13th, 1836. He supplied the pulpit to July 17th, 1845. July 31st, 1845, Rev. Theron Loomis was invited to preach; concluded his labors Sept. 7th, 1846.

Rev. Thomas Dutton was invited April 29th, 1847; closed his labors, Sept., 1851. Mr. Dutton was succeeded by Rev. Mr. Merritt. He supplied the pulpit, in part, from Dec., 1851, to May, 1852. Records are not definite. May 24, 1852, Rev. Mr. Fletcher was invited; remained the minister until Oct. 2d, 1854. I came to this Church June 1st, 1855. Rev. Messrs. Dutton, Coltrin and others supplied the desk from the time of Mr. Fletcher's departure until my coming.

16. *Notice of the Church of Montebello, Hancock county, Illinois, by Br.* JOHN MORSE, *member.*—The First Congregational Church of Montebello was organized April 19th, 1849, with nine members, three males, William Donald, A. H. Levings, John Morse, and six females. Of these, seven were from other Churches, and two united by profession. Rev. Joseph Mason preached for the Church some six months, who was succeeded by Rev. John Rankin, of Warsaw, in 1850, half of the time. During 1851, the Rev. Mr. Henry labored with us some three or four months, half the time.

The first of October, 1851, we called a meeting of all the friends of Christ, feeling that something must be done to secure, if possible, the labors of some one of Christ's ministers, who should reside among us, which resulted in obtaining the Rev. William C. Merritt to become our Pastor, in the Spring of 1852. Rev. Mr. Merritt remained the Pastor ot this Church until August 17th, 1856. During his ministry there were added to the Church thirty-six members, twenty-one by letter, and fifteen by profession. The Church built a house of worship during the years 1854 and 1855.

In Oct., 1856, the Church invited the Rev. Joseph Mason, of Alton, Ill., to become their minister. Rev. Mr. Mason remained until the 19th of February, 1859. During this time, there were nine accessions to the Church, three by profession and six by letter.

There were such changes in the Doctrinal views of Mr. Mason, as led to his removal. The Church was greatly discouraged and distressed by the condition of things, and, for many months, languished, and was ready to die. At length, the Lord of the harvest sent Rev. E. N. Bartlett, who had been laboring in Kidder, Mo., and was driven out by the rebellion, under whose ministrations, since the early part of 1861, the Church has been revived and strengthened.

17. *Notice of the Church in Newtown, Adams county, Illinois, by Rev.* S. HOPKINS EMERY, *of Quincy.*—Having failed of a notice of this Church, on application to its membership, and other ministers, who might be supposed to know more of its history, it remains only to state that it was organized, according to the minutes of the General Association, in January, 1852, and that its present membership is not far from thirty.

Rev. George J. Barrett preached for the Church nearly three years, and its supply has been irregular and partial the rest of the time. Among others, Rev. George W. Williams, of Beverly, preached for them one year. They are supplied with a very comfortable place of worship, and being located in a rich agricultural region, there is no reason why the Church should not, with God's blessing, live and prosper.

18. *Notice of the Church in Payson, Adams county, Illinois, by Br.* J. K. SCARBOROUGH, *member.*—The Congrega-

tional Church of Payson was organized May 8th, 1836, with twenty members. Rev. Anson Hubbard, who had previously been preaching in the place, continued as stated supply till the expiration of the year. About May 1st, 1857, Rev. Thomas Cole was invited to supply the pulpit for one year, which he continued to do as stated supply till July 29th, 1838, when he was installed as pastor, which position he retained till May 1st, 1841. During the former part of Mr. Cole's ministry, the Church received large accessions, but was diminished January, 1839, by the withdrawal of twenty members for the purpose of forming a Presbyterian Church at Newtown. A new and (for those times) expensive church building was dedicated near the close of his ministry, in March, 1841. Rev. Z. K. Hawley supplied the pulpit from July 1st, 1841, to Oct., 1842. On the 18th of Nov., 1842, the Church building was burned, leaving the Church without a house and without a pastor, in the severest financial pressure, and in debt for the construction of the house destroyed. For nearly a year, the Church were without regular preaching and, for more than that time, were compelled to hold their meetings in school houses or such other places as could, from time to time, be procured, the result of which was a diminution of numbers to about one half. Gloomy times those, and in September, 1843, Rev. J. H. Prentiss was employed as stated supply, and continued so to labor till September, 1851. During the years 1843 and 1844, a house, much smaller and less expensive than the former, was erected, which still remains. Dec. 1, 1851, Rev. Z. K. Hawley was again employed as stated supply, and remained four years, till Dec. 1. 1855. Our present minister, Rev. Cephas A. Leach, commenced his labors Aug. 1, 1856. The Church has been prospered during his ministry.

19. *Notice of the Church in Pittsfield, Pike county, Illinois, by Rev.* WILLIAM CARTER, *Minister.*—The Church in Pittsfield was organized January 1st, 1837, by Rev. **A. T.** Norton, with five members, after the Presbyterian form. Mr. Norton had charge of the Church until the Spring of 1838. In Oc-

4

tober, 1838, Rev. Wm. Carter took charge of the Church,
preaching to it one half of the time until Nov., 1847, when
he commenced laboring with it the whole time, which he has
continued to the present. In 1840, the Church enjoyed for
the first time a revival of religion. From that time, the
Church has had frequent seasons of religious interest, eleven
in all, at each of which it has received valuable additions, as
the result. The whole number received into the Church is
three hundred and ninety-two ; by letter, eighty-one; on
profession, three hundred and eleven. The number of members, April 1st, 1860, was two hundred and twenty-six—absent ten.

In March, 1841, the Church assumed the Congregational
form, with but one dissenting vote. It has aimed to carry
out the true Congregational principle of receiving all whom
we had reason to believe the Lord Jesus Christ has received,
if they wished to unite with us. We have therefore required
assent only to the fundamental doctrines of the Bible, which
all evangelical denominations hold in common, and have allowed liberty of conscience as to the mode of baptism, and
the baptism of infants. We have received to our fellowship
those who had been Baptists, Methodists, Old and New School
Presbyterians, Lutherans, Moravians, Associate Presbyterians, and Roman Catholics. Nor have there ever been any
divisions in the Church touching doctrine. Few Churches,
it is believed, have been more united among themselves than
this Church. It has also endeavored to cultivate friendly re-
lations with all other Churches of our Lord. In our early
history, we held protracted meetings with our Methodist
brethren and with our Baptist brethren, until they thought
it best to hold them separately. Whilst we had preaching
but half the time, we gladly allowed each of those denominations the use of our house of worship, until they built for
themselves.

20. *Notice of the First Congregational Church, Quincy,
Adams county, Illinois, by Rev. S. HOPKINS EMERY, Minister.*
—The First Congregational, which was also the first Church

of any name organized* in Quincy, consisted, in its beginning,
of seven males and eight females, viz: Amos Bancroft and
Mrs Adelia Bancroft, Rufus Brown and Mrs. Nancy Brown,
Peter Felt and Mrs. Mary Felt, Henry H. Snow and Mrs.
Lucy K. Snow, Levi Wells and Mrs. Anna Wells, Mrs. Maria
Robbins, wife of John P. Robbins, Mrs. Margaret Rose, wife
of Jeremiah Rose, Mrs. Martha Turner, wife of Rev. Asa
Turner, Daniel Henderson, Hans Patten. These fifteen, on
Saturday, the 4th of December, 1830, subscribed unto the
Lord in this city, then seven years old, and a place of only a
few houses. It was one of these houses, Peter Felt's, on the
south-west corner of Maine and Fourth, which answered the

* My valued friend, Deacon Willard Keyes, one of the original settlers
of Quincy, and earliest members of this Church, has furnished the following notice of a good man and faithful minister, whose labors prece-
ded, and doubtless prepared the way for the organization of this Church:

Rev. Jabez Porter, of Mass., came to Quincy, I think in 1828, in search
of health. He taught a small school in the log Court House, on the S. E.
corner of the Public Square, which was also used for preaching and Sunday Schools in those early times of Quincy.

He was a good man, and sought opportunities of promoting the cause
of Christ. I accompanied him one Sabbath ten or twelve miles south, to
preach in a school house near Fall Creek. The audience was not large,
as the settlement was sparse and had been accustomed to Methodist
preaching, if they had any, which was seldom. It was from him I first
heard of the Temperance movement in New England, and entered into
an argument with him—for I was at that time in partnership with a
man building a distillery—not thinking it any more immoral business
than raising corn or potatoes. Almost every one drank when they could
get it. I argued there would be just as much made and drank whether I
made any or not. I admitted there was need of reform—but did not
think much would be effected in reclaiming drunkards, who I supposed
were the only class that needed laboring with. He brought many strong
arguments and facts to sustain his position, and closed by wishing I
could read the publications issuing from Andover on the subject. Although I defended a bad cause as well as I could, the discussion, I trust,
had a salutary effect on my mind.

However, the distillery went on to completion, and they made part of
a barrel of stuff they called whisky, when my partner, who was the active man in the business, was suddenly prostrated by sickness and died!
I had no heart to prosecute the business farther, and willingly suffered
the whole to go to destruction. My loss was about $1,000, at which I
rejoiced, hoping it was the penalty for my complicity in the matter. I
have digressed from my narrative to relate my whisky experience.

Mr. Porter's health continued to decline, but his last days on earth
experienced the kind nursing and Christian sympathy of Mrs. Jeremiah
Rose, at whose house he was permitted to close his eyes in peace, and enter upon his Heavenly rest, in August or September, 1829, as I think.—
He left his Bible—as his dearest earthly treasure—with Mr. Rose's
family. He lies buried on what is now known as Jefferson Square.

purpose of a sanctuary on this memorable Saturday—and it
was sufficiently large. It was the honored home of the first
Christian Church in Quincy, on the day of its organization.
Of these fifteen members, four had been members of Congre-
gational Churches, four of Presbyterian Churches, three of
Baptist, and four united by profession. Rev. Asa Turner*

* FROM REMINISCENCES OF DEACON KEYES.—Rev. Asa Turner, Jr., of
Templeton, Mass., with his then young wife, who before marriage was
Miss Martha Bull, of Hartford, Conn., came to Quincy in Nov, 1830, as a
missionary sent out by the American Home Miss. Society to Illinois, in
connection with some eight or ten other young ministers. I will mention
some of their names, as I recollect them: Albert Hale, John M. Ellis,
Wm. Kirby, Elisha Jenny, Solomon Hardy, William Carter, Flavel Bas-
com, Aratus Kent, Julian M. Sturtevant. Some of these were associated
with Dr. Beecher, in charge of Illinois College.
    Rev. Asa Turner, Jr., organized the first Church in Quincy, December
4th, 1830—seven males and eight females, total fifteen—in name "Presbyterian," but in every other sense Congregational. October 10th, 1833,
changed the name to Congregational by unanimous vote of the Church.
Mr. Turner remained a most efficient and faithful pastor of the First
Congregational Church of Quincy until June, 1838. Seldom a communion
but some were added to the Church. If strangers came into the place,
he was the first to find them out and lead them to church; but not to
proselyte to his Church. He was very friendly with other denominations, and often advised to connect with other Churches where their connection or previous training might lead them. He was unsectarian, as
witness the first five articles of "Regulations and Articles of Faith and
Covenant" of the First Congregational Church, Quincy, Ill. These were
drawn up by him at the organization of the Church, in December, 1830.
    He was very faithful with young converts, inspiring them with confi-
dence to speak and pray in prayer meeting and the family. The Church
prospered under his pastoral care. In 1834, I think, the Church voted to
dispense with aid from the Home Missionary Society in paying his salary,
and commenced repaying what they had received in former years. Mr.
Turner asked for a dismission the first of June, 1838, to the regret of a
large majority of the Church.
    Influential men out of the Church testified that Mr. Turner had done
more in promoting the prosperity of Quincy than any other man.
    Rev. Solomon Hardy, (Pres.,) supplied our Church in the summer of
1833, while Mr. Turner and family visited East. I am uncertain of his
place of nativity—a man of rather feeble health, but, I think, a faithful
minister, his wife a Miss Barton, of Jacksonville, an estimable lady.
Mr. Hardy, on seeing the records of our Church, said if we sent such
records up to Presbytery they would be sent back at once, as they were
Congregational, and nothing Presbyterian about them. It was this re-
mark, perhaps, that stimulated our Church, on the return of Mr. Turner,
to change our name to Congregational, before exposing our ignorance of
Presbyterianism. Mr. Hardy preached for a year or two for the Mendon
Congregational Church, and then went, I think, to the Northern part of
the State, where he died many years ago.
    Rev. David Nelson preached frequently for us after Mr. Turner left.
He was a strong minded man in his maturity, but was now failing—the
author of "Cause and Cure of Infidelity." He had been a strong infidel
until middle life—was a surgeon in the army of 1812-15. He was a na-

and Rev. Cyrus L. Watson were present, and aided in the organization. They called their Church Presbyterian, but unanimously changed the name, to correspond with their actual polity in practice, the 10th of October, 1833. Of the fifteen original members, six are probably deceased. Three remain as members of this Church, three are members of the Center Church, one was an original member of the Congregational Church in Fontenelle, N. T., one remains a member of the First Presbyterian Church in this city, with which she united at its formation, and one is a member of the Congregational Church in Denmark, Iowa.

This Church was able to erect an humble edifice for the worship of God, in 1832, called on the records their meeting house, but which men of the world, somewhat derisively, were wont to style the "Lord's Barn." But whether a barn or

tive of Tennessee, but on his conversion, he renounced slavery on conscientious scruples, and in consequence was driven from Missouri to Illinois. He was the originator of Mission Institutes, or a plan for self-educating Missionaries. He died in 1841, and lies buried in Woodland Cemetery.

Rev. Moses Hunter, Principal of Mission Institute No. 2, at what is now called East Quincy, preached often for our Church, after the removal of Mr. Turner—a most excellent, but somewhat eccentric man, quite original in his mode of thought and action. He was from Western New York. Hearing of Dr. Nelson's plan of training Missionaries, he came here to examine the plan, and entered upon establishing Mission Institute No. 2, deviating in some things from Dr. Nelson's plan. He died at Chicago, on his way East on business for the Institute, in 1843.

Rev. Charles Stewart Renshaw preached for the First Congregational Church from July, 1838, to February, 1839. He was a native of Georgia, and a nephew of Commodore Charles Stewart—held a midshipman's warrant in U. S. N. under Com. Stewart—visited Sandwich Islands and other parts of the world with his uncle, and from his own statement was a dissolute young man until his conversion, which, I think was in Philadelphia. He gave up his commission in the Navy, and repaired to Oberlin to prepare for preaching the Gospel. After graduating at Oberlin, he found a wife among the female graduates. They started in the Spring of 1838 to go to Oregon as Missionaries, but arrived at Independence, Mo., the starting place of the caravan which they were to accompany, three days too late. They attempted to follow, but could not overtake them. His wife engaged in teaching at a Methodist Missionary station among the Indians in Kansas, and he returned, in company with a young man from Mission Institute, here. He engaged to preach for our Church for six months. His wife joined him in December.

Mr. Renshaw afterwards went as a Missionary, under the American Miss. Association, to the Island of Jamaica, and spent several years among the emancipated blacks, but returned to the U. S. a few years since on account of his health, and I believe has since died.

something better, it is sufficient that when the books are opened, "it shall be said, This and that man was born in her, and the Highest Himself shall acknowledge it." This meeting house, which answered an excellent purpose till it was superseded in 1842 by our present house, may still be seen,* at least the toppling ruins, contiguous to Mr. Felt's house, removed near the alley on Fourth, between Jersey and Maine. The Church had also a camp ground of ten acres, near the present residence of Mr. Jameson, where protracted and mass meetings were at times held. The fruits of such special services were gathered in large numbers into the Church. During Rev. Mr. Turner's ministry of seven years, and a little more, two hundred and forty-four persons were received to the Church, but, as proof of the rapidity with which changes are brought about in this Western country, by death and removal, only twenty-four of this large number still continue with us. Of the whole number, one hundred and sixteen were received on profession, one hundred and twenty-eight by letter. Of the two hundred and twenty-four, not now of our number, who rejoiced to call Rev. Mr. Turner their pastor, some, doubtless, are awaiting his coming in Heaven—while the greater part, we trust, are strengthening many a Church in diverse sections, both West and East.

The year 1839, when the Church had no pastor, was not a witness to any large increase of membership. It was rather diminished. The protracted meeting held on Rev. Horatio Foote's coming to the place, gathered into the Church a large number—sixty-nine, during the year 1840. During the seven years and a half of Mr. Foote's ministry, one hundred and seventy-three were received to the Church—ninety-eight by profession, seventy-five by letter. Of this number, thirty retain their membership in the Church, furnishing still further evidence of the mutation of human affairs, and how rapidly Churches change, and like the human body, lose the particles of which they were originally composed, but retain their identity.

---

* Since this writing it has quite disappeared.

In 1847, when again deprived of a pastor, few were added to the Church, and then, as at other times during its history, the foundation of other Churches was laid in the loss of some of its most valued members. This work of founding other Churches commenced early. I will revert to it again.

Rev. Rollin Mears* was with the Church not far from five years. During this time, fifty-two united with it, twenty-nine by profession, twenty-three by letter, and of these eleven only continue members. Another vacancy, and then Rev. Mr. Potter was minister for a time, during which twenty-five united, eighteen by profession and seven by letter, of whom ten "remain to this present."

Thus we are brought down to the time of the present pastor's settlement, in the latter part of 1855, and during these seven years, the Lord has added unto us one hundred and twenty-two, thirty-nine by profession, and eighty-three by letter, of whom sixty-three are still members of the Church, and residing within reach of our place of worship. A few others of the number are temporarily absent. Of the present resident members of the Church, nearly one-half have become members during the seven years of our pastorate. Notwithstanding our strenuous efforts to dispose of the names of absentees—ninety-nine such cases having been disposed of in December of 1858, more than fifty who are nominal members of our Church are absent from us, some of them however only for a short season. That those who have been dropped from our list are not lost to the Kingdom of Christ, appears from the fact that almost every Church in this city and the vicinity has received accessions, and in many instances original members, from this Church.† Thus early as 1833, Deacon Chit-

---

* A more particular notice of Mr. Mears will be found on a subsequent page.

† FROM REMINISCENCES OF DEACON KEYES.—Several ministers and ministers' wives have gone out from this Church, of whom the following names occur to me: Rebecca Morgan studied at Oberlin, married Rev. C. S. Cady, who preached for a time at Barry, and is now laboring in Iowa. Jane Ballard married Rev. John Rendall, Missionary of the American Board of Com. for Foreign Missions, to Madura, India. Elizabeth Ballard married Rev. Therou Loomis, now settled in Wisconsin.

tenden and wife left with others to plant a Church in Mendon. In 1837, twenty or more were dismissed to form a Church at the Mission Institute, and assist in organizing a Methodist Church in Quincy. In 1840, not far from twenty left to become the nucleus of a Presbyterian interest in the city. Again in 1847, about fifty colonized as the Centre Congregational Church. In 1856, a small number received letters, who organized the 2d Congregational Church in Nebraska Territory. In 1859, the new Churches in Beverly, Dallas City, Hamilton, Ill., and Hannibal, Mo., each received one or more members who were once connected with us.— Thus the Lord permits our members, transferred to other fields of labor, to lay the foundations of many generations. If they be well laid, this is no small privilege surely—even if in so doing, we are called to suffer loss. This affiliation of membership should be an indissoluble bond of union with these sister Churches, which have sprung, as it were, out of our loins. "For no man ever yet hated his own flesh, but nourished it and cherished it, even as the Lord the Church. For we are members of His body, of His flesh and of His bones" —members also one of another.

21. *Notice of the Center Congregational Church, Quincy, Adams County, Illinois, by Rev.* NORMAN A. MILLARD, *Min-*

Maria Ballard married Rev. William E. Holyoke, now of Polo. These sisters, daughters of Deacon Elijah Ballard, were all educated at the Mission Institute. Elizabeth Safford married Rev. Adin H. Fletcher, who went to India, as Missionary with Mr. Rendall, but returned on account of ill health. Catharine Stoby married Rev. Mr. Jones, Missionary to Jamaica. Jane Stoby married Rev. James Weller, also a member of this Church, now pastor of a Congregational Church in this State. Celestia Brown married Rev. Silas Francis, also a member of this Church, and both are living in Nebraska Territory. Mrs. Bethiah Beardsley, wife of Rev. William Beardsley, was a member of this Church. Also, Mrs. M. G. Apthorp, wife of Rev. William P. Apthorp. Also, Mrs. Ann M. Nichols, wife of Rev. Warren Nichols. Rev. Joseph T. Holmes and wife, Rev. Alfred C. Garrett and wife, Rev. Charles Burnham. Rev. William Mellen, Missionary to Africa, Rev. George R. Moore, Rev. James A. Dunn, were also connected with the Church. To these may be added, Rev. Hiram P. Roberts and wife—and Rev. Ruel M. Pierson, if not a member of the Church, encouraged to enter the ministry, and aided in the preparatory course by the pastor, Rev Mr. Turner, and its membership.

The above record is made that it may appear this Church has not been altogether neglectful of its duty in providing a ministry for the West.

ister.—The Centre Congregational Church of Quincy was organized August 1st, 1847. It was believed as the city was very considerably increasing in population, and demanded more churches, that two churches of our order were required and that, under existing circumstances, more good could thus be done to the cause of Christ, both at home and abroad.

The number of members at the organization was forty. The whole number of members to this date has been two hundred and thirteen. The present number is one hundred and thirty-nine. Frequent interesting revivals of religion have blessed the Church during its existence, and additions to it have been mostly from conversions in revivals on profession of faith. During the work of grace with which the city was blessed in the year 1860, a larger number was added to this Church than in any other year during its existence. Centre Church has from the beginning entered heartily into all the benevolent movements and reforms of the day. Its members have been especially devoted to the interests of Sabbath Schools, and many of the children and youth have been led to the Savior. The house of worship of this Church is a neat and commodi-ous edifice, erected at a cost of $15,000. It is furnished with a good bell and organ, and has convenient rooms for Prayer Meetings, Sabbath Schools, and Pastor's Study. The Society is now making an effort to pay its indebtedness, with encouraging prospects of success.

Rev. Horatio Foote had charge of the Church from its organization until the beginning of the year 1861, when he resigned, but continued to supply the pulpit for a few months, after which the Church was without a stated Minister until September, 1862, when Rev. Norman A. Millerd, the present Minister, was engaged to labor with them.

22. *Notice of the German Congregational Church, Quincy, Adams Co., Illinois, by Rev.* CHARLES EDWARD CONRAD, *Minister.*—My beginning in Quincy, Ill., was in January, 1858, in the court-house—gathering together the poor, scattered fragments of what we may call a Church catastrophe; and even this, though being done with anxious labors, and praying day

and night, would seem, for a long time, as a failure; because the materials thus found would not fit and join together, until, at last, succeeding in July, when a congregation of nine members was formed according to the rules of an organization. Since that time we went on, building a meeting-house on credit, or better, in the trust upon the Lord, and joined, at the spring meeting held in the First Congregational Church at Quincy, 1860, the Congregational body of the Illinois Association. Now may we confess to the glory of God, that the Lord has blessed us, though under great hardships, tribulations and heavy labors. We continue still; and though but very slowly, yet we grow; yea, and I dare say that our little Church has been, in many respects, a greater blessing to the German population in Quincy and about, than many will bear account of; because our controversial neighbors, who had become almost drowsy, were challenged by it to emulations. Enmity and envy, indeed, have been able, hitherto, to keep us down below what we might have been without such things in this world; yet we are a Church of Christ, and though we number not three and five thousands, still we are Christ's company. The following will show our condition and present state:

Church organization, of nine members, taking place July, 1858; received into the Church since, on confession, 58; deceased in Christ, 3; dismissed in honor by letters, 10; by excommunication, 2; and of a free, willing departure, 2; thus leaving fifty in membership, of which number four are now absent, some of them serving their country in the army. Those who left us for other places, live with us in good harmony, and it is hoped the blessings received by means of our congregation and its instrumentality will follow them through all their lives, and perhaps it may prove a blessing to those with whom they have come in closer connection.

23. *Notice of the Church in Rockport and Atlas, Pike Co., Ill., by Rev.* SAMUEL R. THRALL, *Minister.*—The Congregational Church of Rockport and Atlas, was organized by Rev. Asa Turner, November, 1834. Rev. Warren Nichols took charge of the Church soon after its organization, and contin-

ued with it some two years. About 1837, Rev. A. T. Norton
had charge of it for a season. During this time it was
changed to a Presbyterian Church. From October, 1838, to
November, 1847, Rev. Wm. Carter had charge of the Church,
preaching to it at different points, one-half the time. During
this period the Church increased from ten or twelve members to
one hundred. Since then, it has been much diminished by
removals and death. On the 17th of March, 1844, the members of the Church, self-moved, changed its organization back
to Congregational, with great unanimity, only one man dissenting, and he readily yielding to the wishes of the majority.
Rev. Gideon C. Clark took charge of the Church in November,
1847, and labored with it two years and a half. Rev. A. H.
Fletcher labored in the Church one year and a half, commen-
cing in the fall of 1850. From April, 1853, Rev. C. S. Cady had charge of the Church for two years. Rev. G. J. Barrett preached to the Church from May, 1856, to March, 1859.
Rev. S. R. Thrall commenced his labors with the Church on
the 1st of March, 1859. It is now called the Church of
Rockport and Summer Hill.

24. *Notice of the Round Prairie Church at Plymouth, Hancock County, Illinois, by Rev.* WILLIAM A. CHAMBERLIN, *Minister.*—The Round Prairie (Plymouth) Congregational Church
was organized January 6, 1836. Seventeen were received
from other Churches, and seven united by profession. A
meeting-house was erected the following year. For some
years, preaching was enjoyed but a part of the time, and the
pulpit was supplied by a number of Ministers. Up to 1845,
the following Ministers had labored in the field:

Rev. Messrs. Wm. Kirby, Anson Hubbard, G. C. Sampson, Z.
K. Hawley, C. E. Murdock, —— Austin, and Wm. C. Rankin.

In 1845, Rev. Milton Kimball became stated supply, and
continued his labors until 1850, though he was not a resident
pastor.

Rev. N. P. Coltrin was pastor from November, 1851, to
September, 1857; and Rev. Wm. B. Atkinson from January,
1858, to January, 1861.

The present pastor, Rev. Wm. A. Chamberlin, commenced his labors in June, 1861, and was ordained and installed Sept. 19th of the same year.

Though at times under the cloud, the Church has not been forgotten by God, and several reviving seasons have been granted unto it.

Owing to various causes, it has not felt able to dispense with help from the Home Missionary Society, until the present year. Number of members, ninety-two. The house of worship now occupied was dedicated July 28th, 1855.

Sullivan Searl was elected Deacon, Aug. 25th, 1836. Resigned May 2d, 1858.

Nathan F. Burton was elected Deacon, Feb. 8th, 1851.

Wm. Holland was elected Deacon, Nov. 2d, 1857.

The present prospects of the Church are encouraging.

25. *Notice of the Church in Wythe, Hancock Co., Ill., by Rev.* SAMUEL DILLEY,* *Minister.*—The Congregational Church of Wythe was organized at the residence of Dr. Griswold, on the 21st of December, 1851, with twenty members.

The first Minister, Rev. George J. Barrett commenced his labors with its organization, and closed April 1st, 1855.

The second, Rev. T. H. Johnson, commenced May, 1855, and closed October 1st, 1856.

The third, Rev. Wm. B. Atkinson, commenced October 1st, 1856, and closed October 1st, 1857.

The fourth, Samuel Dilley, began his labors April 1, 1858.

The Church has enjoyed three revivals—the first at the time of its organization, the second in the winter of 1853, which resulted in the addition of eleven members ; the third occurred in the winter of 1856, and added twelve members to the congregation of believers.

There was a schism in the Church in 1855, which resulted in the loss of a number of influential and useful members.

On the 1st of September, 1854, a neat and comfortable place of worship, costing $1,400 was dedicated.

*NOTE BY THE COMPILER.—Rev. Mr. Dilley has left; and his place is supplied by Rev. N. P. Coltrin, formerly of Plymouth and Griggsville.

In June, 1858, a comfortable parsonage, costing, with the lot, about $800, was completed and occupied.

The church is out of debt. Present number of members forty.

One Unassociated Church and Churches, whose connection with the Association has ceased.—The Congregational Church at Fowler Station, a few miles from Mendon, Adams county, was organized Tuesday, November 26th, 1861, and is not yet associated, although it will probably apply for membership at the next meeting of the Association. Several Churches have had a connection with the Association, which now belong elsewhere, as the Churches of Jacksonville, Warsaw, Woodburn, Waverly, Beardstown, and Denmark, Iowa, and a few have become extinct. These last are St. Mary, Long Grove, Woodville, Mission Institute No. 1, Monmouth, Panther Creek, Cass county. The Church in Hillsgrove is ready to be added to their number.

NOTICES OF DECEASED MINISTERS OF THE IL-LINOIS ASSOCIATION.

1. *Notice of Rev.* JOSEPH T. HOLMES, *by Rev. S. Hopkins Emery, of Quincy.*—Rev. Joseph Tourtelott Holmes was a descendant, on his mother's side, from the French. His maternal grandfather Tourtelott took great interest in the religious welfare of the family. Joseph was one of thirteen children, ten of whom reached adult age. He was born of Stephen and Mary Holmes, in Thompson, Ct., Nov. 15, 1806. His parents were not professors of religion, but, in their external life, exemplary, training their household well. The father died a year or two since; the mother is still living. They sacrificed much for the education of their children, expending not less than a thousand dollars for the education of each child.

Mr. Holmes became a christian, it is thought, when about sixteen, although living at a distance from any Church privileges. It was not until three years afterwards, when he left home for Manchester, Ct., where he had charge of some mercantile and manufacturing business, that he took a decided position as a Christian, and professed religion, uniting with the Congregational Church in that place. He at once became Superintendent of the Sabbath School, and an efficient promoter of every good cause. He had a strong desire for the Christian Ministry at this time, but the way to secure an education seemed hedged up — besides, he was fearful that his health was not sufficient. He remained five years in Manchester, where he married* Mary Ann, daughter of Pardon Brown, Esq., of Glastenbury, Ct., May 13, 1830. In July, 1834, he removed with his family to the West, and in October of the following year located in Quincy, Ill., with the hope of promoting their temporal and spiritual interest. He continued in the same business as in the East, but unlike some professors of religion, who make such a removal, did not leave his profession and living exemplification of religion behind him. He at once united with the First Congregational Church in Quincy, even before the removal of his family, and soon after was elected Deacon, which office he filled with great acceptance to the time of his resignation in 1838. He was a firm supporter of the Ministry during these years—a man upon whose counsel, and large measure of common sense, and Christian integrity, the Minister and the members of the church greatly relied. All this time there was an intense longing within his breast,

---

*The children by this marriage were as follows:

1. Frederic Brown, born April 13, 1831, died Jan. 28, 1853. This son united with the Griggsville Church in 1845, giving good evidence of piety at a much earlier age. He taught in the Deaf and Dumb Institution at Jacksonville. It was his purpose to become a Minister, but health failed. He gave promise of great usefulness.

2. Joseph Tourtelott, born Oct. 29, 1834.

3. Emily, born Aug. 30, 1836, died Aug. 30, 1845. This daughter died a triumphant Christian death at such an early age. She was sick three weeks, during which time she anticipated death joyfully, saying she desired to go and be with Jesus. She gave her Bible to her physician, a skeptical man, saying she hoped to meet him in Heaven.

4. William Pardon, born May 12, 1839, died July — 1839.

5. Stephen Stone, born March 8, 1841.

Two sons and the widowed mother survive—the latter having consecrated herself with singular self-sacrifice, and zeal to the good of the soldiers, in the Hospitals of Springfield, Mo. during the winter of 1862-3. The only likeness of the deceased was unfortunately lost by an artist, who had it temporarily in his possession.

to preach the Gospel. He seemed to hear a voice saying: "Woe is me if I preach *not* the Gospel." This voice at length prevailed. He left a lucrative business, at his present advanced age, resumed classical studies, to which he had attended in his youth, was licensed by the Illinois Association, Oct. 16, 1841, and after this, pursued a theological course in New Haven, Ct. On his return West, he was soon called to become Pastor of the Church in Griggsville, Ill., having first received ordination by the Illinois Association at its meeting in Quincy. The call was unanimous, and the union was a growing one till the time of his death, April 13, 1847. The Church was greatly strengthened during his brief Ministry of three and a half years. His last sickness was a rapid and raging fever, of two weeks continuance, which deprived him of reason a part of the time. During the lucid intervals, his mind was altogether on heavenly things. Once he desired his family to be collected together, and said: "I want you to read the chapter about the cleansing of Naaman, the Syrian," naming the place where it was to be found. He then, with considerable exertion and deep feeling, knelt down and prayed with his wife and children, offering up such fervent supplications for himself and them as could never be forgotten. "The rest of Heaven seems sweet and glorious," he said at another time. Although he felt that his family needed him, he desired the Lord's will to be done. His death occurred soon after the meeting* of the Illinois Association at Quincy, as an entry on the Minutes, bearing date April 10, 1847, indicates: "Bro. Carter, having received information that the family of our Bro. Holmes earnestly desire his presence, that he may sympathize with them in their affliction, requested leave of absence

---

*The last writing he ever did was the preparation of the statistics of the Griggsville Church for that meeting.

Bro. Holmes was Clerk of the meeting of Delegates of the Congregational Churches of Illinois, assembled at the house of Rev. Asa Turner, in Quincy, Nov. 28, 1834, to consider the question of organizing an Association, and to take the initiatory steps. He was also Scribe of the Convention which organized the General Association in 1844, and Moderator of its annual meeting in 1846, when he preached the Associational Sermon from Matt. 5: 14.

for this purpose." Rev. Mr. Carter preached the funeral sermon.

The writer of this notice has been permitted to read sermons of the deceased brother, preached in 1845–6, from the following texts: Matt. 28; 19, 20: "Go ye therefore, and teach all nations, baptising them in the name of the Father, and of the Son, and of the Holy Ghost."

Rom. 3: 28. "Therefore we conclude that a man is justified by faith, without the deeds of the law."

Gal. 6: 14: "But God forbid, that I should glory, save in the cross of our Lord Jesus Christ."

The plan of a discourse, or rather discourses, which he was not permitted to complete, now lies before me—the last labor of his intellect and heart on earth. He entered upon the treatment of a mighty theme, which has been opened up before him in the Heavenly world as it could never have been here. Text—Titus 3, 5: "Not by works of righteousness which we have done, but according to his mercy he saved us by the washing of Regeneration, and renewing of the Holy Ghost."

After remarking that the great idea in the mind of the Apostle in this passage, is the *work wrought in the sinner, that he might be saved*, he proceeds to announce his subject—the doctrine of *Regeneration*—dividing it as follows:

1. The fact, or reality of Regeneration.
2. Its necessity to salvation.
3. The nature of the work.
4. The agent, and instrument.

He proposes to answer several questions before he closes, as:

1. Is Regeneration instantaneous or progressive?
2. Is the individual active or passive in the work?
3. Is the work partial or complete?

These questions were never answered by him on earth.— They, and many others have been answered to his complete satisfaction long since in heaven. Under the first head of his discourse, the fact or reality of Regeneration, he was about citing the great Apostle, as a witness, when he was called up higher, and permitted to commune with him in glory.

2. *Notice of Rev.* WILLIAM KIRBY, *by Rev.* Z. K. *Hawley, of Macomb*—drawn largely from the sermon of President Sturtevant at the funeral of Mr. Kirby.

Rev. William Kirby was born in Middletown, Connecticut, August 1805, eldest son of Elisha Kirby. Pecuniary circumstances led him in early youth, to Guilford, where, by the avails of his labor, he could enjoy better educational advantages than were otherwise obtainable. During a general religious interest there, he was hopefully converted, and joined the First Congregational Church by profession. Being regarded as a youth of more than ordinary promise, he was enencouraged to enter upon a course of preparation for the ministry. He graduated at Yale College in 1827, with one of the highest honors of his class, and with a marked Christian character. His theological course was pursued at New Haven, and completed in 1831. During this period the subject of Home Missions, in connection with Collegiate Education in the West, assumed a prominent importance in the Institution, resulting in an association of seven students (one of whom was Mr. Kirby) for the prosecution of an original enterprise, which was the origin of ILLINOIS COLLEGE, in which Mr. Kirby became an instructor in 1831, continuing two years with remarkable assiduity and energy. The labor and care required in the management of such an Institution, thus early in the settlement of the State, made so severe drafts upon his constitution as to render a change necessary.

Having married, in 1832, Miss Hannah Wolcott, of Jacksonville—a native of East Windsor, Connecticut—he entered, in the spring of 1833, upon the labors of the ministry, according to his original purpose. His first field was with the church at Union Grove, Putnam county, where he continued a year and a half. This church was composed of very discordant elements, which, excited by the ecclesiastical dissensions of the day, so obstructed his labors as to induce him to seek a more quiet and encouraging sphere of usefulness. This was

6

found at Blackstone's Grove, Will county, in an agricultural community of new settlers. Here Mr. Kirby and family endured a full share of the hardships and privations of frontier life. The barest necessaries were obtainable from abroad only. Wheat flour was only *thought of;* corn meal was procured by a journey of miles, shelling the corn and 'carrying it to a distant mill, after a cost of a dollar and a half a bushel. His nearest post office was at Chicago, twenty-eight miles distant.

The experience of a year and a half proved these labors and privations to be too severe for his previously overtaxed constitution ; while his duties as Trustee of Illinois College— one of the main objects of the Association of which he was a member—was an additional inducement to a change of location ; all of which led to the acceptance of a call of the church and congregation at Mendon, Adams county, to the labors of the ministry among them. He entered this field in 1836, where he pursued his work for nine years—sanctioned by repeated and special outpourings of the Spirit. Under this culture, the church was raised not only to a position of pecuniary independence, but was imbued with those vital principles which will render it a permanent and efficient agency in extending the institutions of the Gospel.

But his peculiar qualifications fitted him for a wider sphere of usefulness, to which he was called in 1845, as General Agent of the American Home Missionary Society in Illinois, —first, for the whole State, and subsequently for the central and southern portions of it. The difficulties, trials and responsibility of that agency, can be but very imperfectly appreciated,. except from experience. Travel was not then performed as it is now, chiefly by Railroads—thus avoiding most tedious labor and serious exposure. Engagements must be kept over bad roads, through unbridged streams, under the scorching heat of summer and against the piercing blasts of winter ; while the " *unrest* " of night was often far more terrible than the fatigue and exposure of the day. But more than these things were " the care of the churches," and the responsibility of the position, between opposite fires kindled by the questions which were dividing the American Home Missionary Society.

Mr. Kirby had opinions, intelligently and conscientiously held, upon Ecclesiastical Polity; but an enlarged Christian catholicism lifted him above the partisan, into a plane entirely above and beyond the corruptions of the narrow-minded sectarian. His principles and his administration were severely judged by those who can hardly ' preach Christ ' without also preaching ' Paul,' or ' Cephas,' or ' Apollos.' Few men, in his position, could have held, with so even a hand, the oscillating balance of party. It is worthy of record, not so much in itself, as from the circumstances—that his last official labor was the special one of founding a *Presbyterian Church.* His life was one continuous sacrifice of self,—a " living sacrifice," upon the altar of Christ. He gave of his pecuniary means largely, in proportion to the amount possessed; but, what was more, *himself*—' a servant of Christ.'

Death found him at his work. " I am ready," said he " to go or stay; I trust I am prepared—I rely not upon the good opinion of others, nor upon anything which I have done. I can truly say, I have no doubts."

He died December 20, 1851, aged 46 years.

3. *Notice of Rev.* ROLLIN MEARS, *by Rev. N. P. Coltrin, of Wythe*—condensed from manuscript of Rev. E. Johnson and a printed obituary by President Sturtevant.

Rollin Mears was born in Bethel, Bond county, Illinois, March 1st, 1821. When he was four years old, his parents removed to Jacksonville, Illinois, where they united with others in forming a Congregational Church, with which Rollin united when he was but twelve years of age. His mother testifies that he gave evidence of conversion in early childhood, and that, without any sudden or marked change, his character appeared to ripen into the full form of Christian faith. Into filial respect and affection were easily grafted reverence and love for God.

At fourteen he entered Illinois College, then in its infancy, and as he pursued his course of study, his companions and teachers discovered in him the true gold of intellectual and moral worth. Soon after his graduation, he became a student in Lane Theological Seminary, where he spent three years. He was licensed to preach at the age of twenty-one. His first year of Ministerial service was at Ottawa, Illinois, after which, to recruit his failing health, he took a sea voyage of a few months to the West Indies. Returning, he became Minister of the Church at Waverly, Illinois, where he remained two years. His next removal was to Quincy, Illinois, where he was married to Miss Laura Savage, and where he ministered for five years and a half to the First Congregational Church. In the social, literary and religious history of that city his name is still recorded and his influence felt for good. In 1853, he was led to accept a call from the Congregational Church in Griggsville, Illinois, and in that year was installed as Pastor. Here, from the outset, his labors were signally blessed; the Church was revived and strengthened—it grew in numbers and graces—built a new house of worship, and breathed a new spirit of life and energy. He was highly respected by the entire people of his community, as a faithful and instructive minister.

His talents were of a high order; his reading extensive and various. As a lecturer on literary and philosophical subjects his thought and style were vigorous, yet classic. His views of Christian doctrine were decidedly evangelical, and he was ardently attached to the Congregational Polity; but he was no sectarian, no religious partisan. He claimed spiritual kindred with all the faithful in Christ, and co-operated with all such in his Master's work. He was a man of prayer—believed much in it himself, and taught the people to prize and practice the same privilege. He died March 28th, 1856, after an illness of nearly two months. Grief spread through his parish with the rumor that he was sick, and deep grief pervaded the community when he was reported as dying. In lucid intervals near his departure, he testified a sure hope and calm confidence in God. He left behind him a widow with two little boys—too young to know that they were written fatherless. His grave,* in the Griggsville cemetery, is marked by a neat monument, erected by his affectionate parishioners.

*NOTE BY THE COMPILER.—I have visited that grave, and sought communion with the spirit of the dear departed brother, whose body sleeps beneath that monument. I never saw him in the flesh, although my predecessor in the pastoral office in Quincy. The memory of him is fresh and fragrant in that place. Said one to me, the other day, who sat beneath his ministry unconcerned in Quincy, whose home is now in Griggsville—" When I read that inscription on his monument—' Remember the words, I spake unto you, when I was yet with you'—I wept at the remembrance of his fidelity, and my thoughtlessness, and solemnly resolved, I would henceforth lead a better life." The well-worn path to the grave is a witness, that one who was beloved in his life, is not forgotten in his death. "He, being dead, yet speaketh."

One of the little boys, referred to above, Charles Edwin, followed his father to the better land, November 7th, 1862. The widowed mother is devoting her time and strength to the good of soldiers' families, in superintending a large sewing establishment on Government work in the city of Quincy.

NOTE BY THE COMPILER.—Our catalogue of past and present ministerial members of the Association may not be complete, through the imperfection of the Records ; but these give the following names of members, as received by vote, from other Ecclesiastical Bodies, or constituted such according to its rules, by receiving ordination from this Body.

MINISTERIAL MEMBERS, BY VOTE, FROM OTHER ECCLESIASTICAL BODIES.

William Carter,	in 1836,	from the Presbytery of Schuyler.	
Anson Hubbard,	"	"	Maine Conference.
Edward Hollister,	"	"	Presbytery of Orange.
William Kirby,	"	"	" " Ottawa.
G. C. Sampson,	in 1837,	"	General Association of Conn.
Asa Turner,	"	"	Presbytery of Schuyler.
Thomas Cole,	in 1838,		also member of Presbytery.
Robert Blake,	"	"	Orange Association.
Reuben Gaylord,	"	"	General Association of Conn.
Zerah K. Hawley,	in 1839,	"	Gen'l Ass'n of N. Hampshire.
Wm. Beardsley,	in 1840,	"	Genessee Consociation, N. Y.
Horatio Foote,	in 1841,	"	Presbytery of Champlain, "
John Ballard,	"	"	" " Cincinnati.
D. R. Williams,	in 1842,	"	Penobscot Association, Maine.
J. H. Prentiss,	in 1844,	"	Fox River Union, Ill.
S. Smith,	in 1847,		
Rollin Mears,	in 1848,	"	" " " "
George J. Barrett,	"	"	Methodist Epis. Conference.
G. C. Clarke,	"	"	Berkshire Association, Mass.
James A. Hawley,	in 1850,	"	Fairfield West Asso'n, Conn.
A. H. Fletcher,	in 1851,	"	Presbytery of Jaffna, Ceylon.
C. S. Cady,	in 1852,		
Timothy Lyman,	"	"	Denmark Association, Iowa.
Z. K. Hawley, 2d time,	1853,	"	Central Association, Illinois
Thomas Waller,	in 1855,	"	Prot. Meth. Conference.
S. Hopkins Emery,	in 1856,	"	Taunton Association, Mass.
Alex. B. Campbell,	"	"	Presbytery of Schuyler, Ill.

Marvin Root,	in 1856,	from the Tolland Co. Association, Conn.
Wm. B. Atkinson,	in 1857,	" " Central Association, Ill.
Cephas A. Leach,	in 1858,	
Samuel Dilley,	"	" " " " "
Samuel R. Thrall,	in 1860,	
Charles E. Conrad,	in 1861,	" " German Evangelical Association of the West.
Enoch N. Bartlett,	in 1863,	From the Gen'l. Assoc'n. of Iowa.
Norman A. Millerd,	"	" " Congregational & Presbyterian Convent'n. of Wis.
William W. Whipple,	"	" " Presbytery of Northern Missouri.

MINISTERIAL MEMBERS BY ORDINATION OF THIS BODY.

Julius A. Reed,*	in 1836,	Licentiate of N. Haven Asso'n., Conn.
William Whittlesey,	in 1837,	" " Hartford " "
Andrew L. Pennoyer,	in 1838,	" " Pres. of Cincinnati.
E. G. Murdock	"	" " N. Haven Assoc., Conn.
Benj. F. Morris,	in 1839,	" " Illinois Association.
Daniel Gavin,	in 1840,	" " Evang. Soc. of Missions, Switzerland.
J. B. Turner,	in 1841,	" " Illinois Association.
J. S. Graves,	in 1843,	" " " "
James R. Dunn,	"	" " " "
Joseph T. Holmes,	"	" " " "
Isaac W. Plumer,	"	
Rollin Mears,	in 1844,	" " " "
Truman M. Post,	"	" " " "
Theron Loomis,	in 1845,	
William C. Merritt,	in 1846,	" " Presby. of Cincinnati.
Joseph Mason,	in 1847,	" " " "
Thomas Dutton,	"	" " New Haven Ass., Conn.
G. B. Hubbard,	in 1848,	" " Hartford Assoc'n., Conn.
J. H. Henry,	in 1850,	
E. H. Gilbert,	"	
Nath. P. Coltrin,	"	
William E. Catlin,	in 1851,	
Henry D. Platt,	"	" " Middlesex Asso'n., Conn.
Thomas H. Johnson,	in 1852,	" " Illinois Association.
George W. Williams,	in 1860,	" " " "
Benj. C. Ward,	"	
J. M. Sturtevant, Jr.,	"	
Wm. A. Chamberlin,	in 1861,	" " Illinois Association.

LICENTIATES OF THE ILLINOIS ASSOCIATION.

Charles Burnham and Benjamin F. Morris,......................in 1838.

Truman M. Post, and J. B. Turner,..........................in 1840.

Seneca Austin, Joseph S. Graves, Joseph T. Holmes, and Rollin Mears,......................................in 1841.

J. R. Dunn,.......................................in 1842.

* Brother Reed writes: "I suppose I was the *first* minister ordained Congregationally in Illinois."

In a letter just received from brother Carter, he says: "It ought to be stated, that Rev. Julius A. Reed, now of Iowa, organized the Church at Carthage, and ministered to it for several years—as also the Church at La Harpe. I aided him in a meeting of a few days, with each of those churches in the winter of 1836."

S. Adams, and A. H. Fletcher,..in 1844.
Thomas Garrick,...in 1846.
Thomas H. Johnson,..in 1850.
Jireh J. Burt,...in 1857.
Dudley B. Eells, and George W. Williams,...........................in 1860.
William A. Chamberlin,..in 1861.

The preceding list may be incomplete, as there are no Records of the Fall meeting of the Association in 1842 at Warsaw, and of the same meeting in 1843, at Quincy. There are other marks of incompleteness, in the early history of the Association. There is no notice, in some cases, of the dismission of ministerial members, who are known to have connected themselves with other Bodies.

The Ministers still belonging to this Body, in the order of time in which they became members, are as follows, with their present field of labor:

Wm. Carter, member in 1836, Minister of the Congregational Church in Pittsfield, Illinois.

Andrew Leeds Pennoyer, member in 1838, Minister of the Congregational Church in La Harpe, Illinois.

Horatio Foote, member in 1841, Chaplain in the Hospitals of Quincy, Illinois.

Nathaniel P. Coltrin, member in 1850, Minister of the Congregational Church in Wythe, Illinois.

Zerah K. Hawley, member in 1853, Minister of the Congregational Church in Macomb, Illinois—absent, at present, visiting the army.

Samuel Hopkins Emery, member in 1856, Minister of the First Congregational Church, Quincy, Illinois.

Alexander B. Campbell, member in 1856, Minister of the Congregational Church in Mendon, Illinois.

Cephas A. Leach, member in 1858, Minister of the Congregational Church in Payson, Illinois.

Samuel Dilley, member in 1858, Minister of the Congregational Church in Chili, Illinois.

Samuel R. Thrall, member in 1858, Minister of the Congregational Church in Summer Hill, Illinois.

George W. Williams, member in 1860, Minister of the Congregational Church in Beverly, Illinois.

Julian M. Sturtevant, Jr., member in 1860, Minister of the Congregational Church in Hannibal, Missouri.

William A. Chamberlin, member in 1861, Minister of the Congregational Church in Plymouth, Illinois.

Charles Edward Conrad, member in 1861, Minister of the German Congregational Church, Quincy, Illinois.

Enoch M. Bartlett, minister in 1863, Minister of the Congregational Churches in Hamilton and Oakwood, Illinois.

Norman A. Millerd, member in 1863, Minister of the Centre Congregational Church, Quincy, Illinois.

William W. Whipple, member in 1863, Minister of the Congregational Church in Griggsville, Illinois.

☞ All the above named brethren were present at the recent meeting (April 2d, 1863,) of the Association in Hannibal, Missouri, with the exception of Messrs Foot, Hawley, Campbell and Conrad—the two first named being engaged in labors among the soldiers, the third absent on a journey East, and the fourth so occupied with meetings in the three Churches, to which he ministers, that he could not be absent for a single day.

The Reports from the Churches were reviving and encouraging. The first meeting of an Ecclesiastical Body of our Denomination in the State of Missouri, occurring at the same time with the meeting of a sister Association—the Congregational Association of Southern Illinois—in St. Louis, was hopeful, as to the future. Friendly Christian greetings were sent to that Body.

Notice was given by brother Dilley, of the Cedron Church, that their name had been changed to Chili, to correspond with the name of the town where it is located. It was, also, voted that the Hillsgrove Church be considered dead, all its members having moved away. The Payson Church, through its Pastor, reported a contribution of seven hundred dollars, the last year, to objects of benevolence, in addition to the Minister's salary of six hundred dollars—making a sum total of thirteen hundred dollars—chiefly from fifteen families, giving an average of over eighty dollars per annum, for religious purposes—an example of liberality worthy of emulation.

TABLE OF CONTENTS.

www.ingramcontent.com/pod-product-compliance
Lightning Source LLC
Chambersburg PA
CBHW032123080426
42733CB00008B/1030